M000095194

Catfulness

Catfulness

The Path to Inner Peace

**Andrews McMeel
Publishing**®

Kansas City · Sydney · London

Andrews McMeel Publishing, LLC
an Andrews McMeel Universal company
1130 Walnut Street, Kansas City, Missouri 64106
www.andrewsmcmeel.com

15 16 17 18 19 TEN 10 9 8 7 6 5 4 3 2 1

ISBN: 978-1-4494-7241-2

Library of Congress Control Number: 2015940907

Compiled *Michael Powell*
Illustrations *Lorenzo Montatore*
Design *Milestone Design*

ATTENTION: SCHOOLS AND BUSINESSES
Andrews McMeel books are available at quantity discounts with bulk purchase for educational, business, or sales promotional use. For information, please e-mail the Andrews McMeel Publishing Special Sales Department: specialsales@amuniversal.com.

Something important is spreading throughout the world: More and more people are discovering the amazing power of catfulness.

Inside this book, dozens of feisty felines reveal the secret to living more catfully.

At home, at work, on the sofa, or lying curled up on top of a radiator, being catful is the way to be.

The first few moments
of the day are some of the
most important as they can
determine the mood for the
rest of the day.

Daniel Willey

Each place is the right
place—the place where
I now am can be
a sacred space.

Ravi Ravindra

The Path to Inner Peace

All happiness depends on a leisurely breakfast.

John Gunther

Seeking is endless.
It never comes to a
state of rest;
it never ceases.

Sharon Salzberg

The Path to Inner Peace

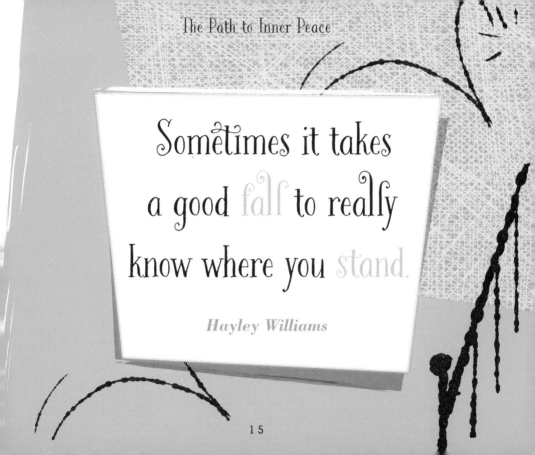

Sometimes it takes
a good fall to really
know where you stand.

Hayley Williams

15

You settle for less, you get less.

Brandi L. Bates

Those not chasing their dreams should stay out of the way of those who are.

Tim Fargo

What greater gift than the love of a cat?

Charles Dickens

The Path to Inner Peace

A fit, healthy body—
that is the best
fashion statement.

Jess C. Scott

There comes a time when you have to choose between turning the page and closing the book.

Josh Jameson

If you clean the floor
with love, you have
given the world
an invisible painting.

Osho

Earthly goods deceive the human heart into believing that they give it security and freedom from worry. But in truth, they are what cause anxiety.

Dietrich Bonhoeffer

All the art of living
lies in a fine mingling
of letting go and
holding on.

Henry Ellis

31

The present moment is filled
with joy and happiness.
If you are attentive,
you will see it.

Thich Nhat Hanh

The Path to Inner Peace

Replace fear of
the unknown with
curiosity.

Danny Gokey

35

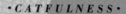

Let one who seeks
not stop seeking until
that person finds.

T. Scott McLeod

The Path to Inner Peace

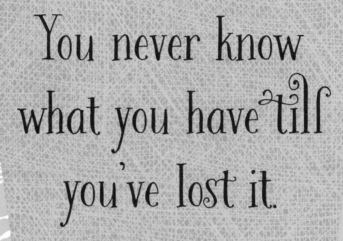

You never know what you have till you've lost it.

Alyson Noël

Turn off your mind,
relax, and float
downstream.

John Lennon

The Path to Inner Peace

If you want to support others you have to stay upright yourself.

Peter Høeg

No matter how thoroughly
you plan, no matter how
much you think you know,
you've never thought
of everything.

John Flanagan

You rest now. Rest for longer than you are used to resting. Make a stillness around you, a field of peace. Your best work, the best time of your life will grow out of this peace.

Peter Heller

Giving connects two people,
the giver and the receiver.
This connection gives birth to
a new sense of belonging.

Deepak Chopra

Whenever you are confronted with an opponent, conquer him with love.

Mahatma Gandhi

Be an opener of doors.

Ralph Waldo Emerson

The Path to Inner Peace

Sometimes your joy is the source of your smile, but sometimes your smile can be the source of your joy.

Thich Nhat Hanh

Trust yourself.
You know more than
you think you do.

Benjamin Spock

The Path to Inner Peace

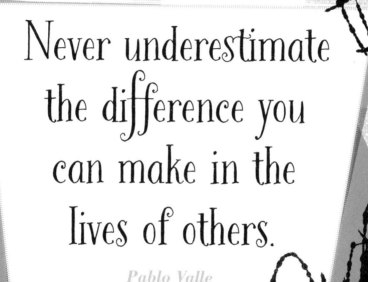

Never underestimate the difference you can make in the lives of others.

Pablo Valle

Do not dwell in the past,
do not dream of the future,
concentrate the mind on
the present moment.

The Teaching of Buddha

The Path to Inner Peace

Sometimes battles are unavoidable.

Shannon A. Thompson

But let there be spaces in your togetherness. And let the winds of the heavens dance between you.

Kahlil Gibran

The Path to Inner Peace

Toxins—better out than in!

Swee Boon Chai

Do not be surprised by
your greatness. . . .
Be surprised that
no one expected it.

Rebecca Maizel

Retire to the center of your being, which is calmness.

Paramahansa Yogananda

Don't believe everything you think. Thoughts are just that–thoughts.

Allan Lokos

Trees are sanctuaries.
Whoever knows how to speak
to them, whoever knows
how to listen to them,
can learn the truth.

Hermann Hesse

If a thing's worth
doing it's worth
doing together.

Michael Bradley

The Path to Inner Peace

Behind every beautiful thing, there's been some kind of pain.

Bob Dylan

There are no accidents. . . .
There is only some
purpose that we haven't
yet understood.

Deepak Chopra

The Path to Inner Peace

82

Collaboration, it turns out, is not a gift from the gods but a skill that requires effort and practice.

Douglas B. Reeves

The first problem of communication is getting people's attention.

Chip Heath and Dan Heath

Rest and be thankful.

William Wordsworth

To make the right choices in life, you
have to get in touch with your soul.
To do this, you need to experience
solitude, which most people are afraid
of, because in the silence you hear
the truth and know the solutions.

Deepak Chopra

The Path to Inner Peace

Sometimes, the simple things are more fun and meaningful than all the banquets in the world.

E. A. Bucchianeri

Whosoever is delighted in solitude, is either a wild beast or a god.

Francis Bacon

The Path to Inner Peace

Cry. Forgive. Learn. Move on. Let your tears water the seeds of your future happiness.

Steve Maraboli